Celebrity Culture

John Drane

the *WayMark* series

Series Editor: David C Searle

Published by
Rutherford House

Copyright © John Drane and Rutherford House
First Published 2005 by Rutherford House
17 Claremont Park, Edinburgh EH6 7PJ
Scotland

The right of John Drane to be identified
as Author of this Work
has been asserted by him
in accordance with the Copyright,
Designs and Patents Act 1988.

British Library Cataloguing in Publication Data

A catalogue record for this book is available from
The British Library

ISBN : 1-904429-08-4

Typeset by David Searle, Edinburgh
and Printed by
T.J. International Ltd., Padstow, Cornwall

Contents

Preface

David and Victoria 'Posh' Beckham we Europeans know, and Princess Diana, Elvis Presley, Madonna and the Beatles much of the world knows, as top-flight celebrities, that class of people whose doings, dead or alive, largely fill the popular media. But were there celebrities in the Bible? Was Jesus in a comparable sense a celebrity? And what relationship is there between celebrity status and sainthood—and our uncanonized evangelical icons like C. S. Lewis and Martyn Lloyd-Jones?

As an interpreter of our culture to contemporary Christians John Drane has developed a most distinctive ministry. This booklet is a model of his art, as he exposes the forces and values at work in our celebrity-dominated world. He analyses it with sensitivity, and challenges Christians, especially Christian teachers and leaders, to direct their energies to engaging with the all-pervasive popular culture which revolves so massively around celebrities, rather than concentrate disproportionately on the apologetic challenge of high-brow culture—Richard Dawkins and his ilk.

Dr Drane serves up education, stimulation, provocation and edification in mixed measure.

Reading short studies on this kind of subject —'tracts for the times', to be sure—should be standard fare for those concerned about the marginalization of Christianity in the West.

David Wright
Edinburgh, 2006

Chapter One

A Brief History of Fame

My wife and I recently travelled from Scotland to Los Angeles. It is a journey we have made many times before, as we both regularly teach in the School of Theology at Fuller Seminary in Pasadena. As we got nearer to our destination, our conversation turned to speculation about what we might have to deal with as we met with the US immigration officers who would scrutinise us before allowing us into their country. We recalled a previous occasion when we were asked if we were married, and the officer on duty had made it plain that she had no time either for married folk or for Christians—and openly expressed regret at the fact that her government had issued us with a visa. Not all employees of the US government are like that, of course, and for every hostile individual we must have met a dozen or more perfectly polite officers who do their job with courtesy and efficiency. But none of our previous experience prepared us for what we actually encountered in April 2005.

Perhaps it was the fact that we were among the first half dozen people off the aircraft, and therefore right at the front of the queue. Maybe it had something to do with the way we were dressed—more formally than most of our friends back home would believe possible! Or just that we had both visited the bathroom before the plane landed, and the weariness of a sixteen hour journey from Scotland had been washed away, at least on the outside. It could also have been that it was late evening in Los Angeles, and this was the last flight to be processed at the end of a long day in which our interrogator had had few light moments.

For whatever reason, when we handed in our passports, the young woman at the desk took one look at my wife, and asked, 'Should I know you? You are so beautiful, you must be someone really famous. Which TV show are you on? Or is it the movies you work in?' As she made these enquiries, her eyes moved back and forth between the picture in my wife's passport and the person standing before her, trying to work out the possible answers to her questions. No amount of explanation about my wife's true identity could convince her that, to us at least, we were just 'ordinary' people. In the end, my wife admitted that she is a published author and was going to speak at a conference for church leaders, which just about made her enough of a celebrity to bring this conversation to a happy ending. The immigration officer told us which church she attended in California, stamped all our papers in double-quick time, and when our bags came through on the priority track we were out of the airport in less than twenty minutes after landing. Andy Warhol memorably said that 'In the future, everybody will be world famous for fifteen minutes.' Maybe this was our fifteen minutes of fame.

A sense of lostness and the search for meaning?

But was there more to it than that? For this woman is typical of millions all over the world, who long for their lives to be touched by 'greatness', even if the reality is more mundane. Is our current obsession with celebrity nothing more than a sign that we are, in Neil Postman's unforgettable phrase, 'amusing ourselves to death'?[1] Or is it a manifestation of something deeper—an indication, perhaps, of a growing sense of our lostness and of a self-conscious search for

---

[1] Neil Postman, *Amusing Ourselves to Death* (New York: Viking, 1985).

meaning, and a desire to be put in touch with some reality that will transcend the ordinary and everyday? In reaching out for celebrities, are we also reaching into the depth of our own souls—and maybe even reaching out for God? And what has any of that to do with Christian spirituality and the mission of the church in the 21st century?

In unpacking this theme, I want first of all to reflect rather briefly on the history of being famous, tracing some common threads from cultures in the ancient world and the way in which they have been incorporated into the social fabric of later times and places.

We will then go on to explore the differences between ancient celebrities and those with whom we are familiar today. This will take us into some well-rehearsed discussions about cultural change, with a particular emphasis on the impact of different forms of mass media in the creation of both modernity and post-modernity and the emergence of stardom in the 20th century.

Finally, there will be some reflections on the spiritual and theological significance of all this in relation to Christian mission and ministry.

Ancient Celebrities[2]

The scenarios might be different, but the impact of celebrities can be traced more or less throughout history, in all cultures and at all times. The remains of ancient civilizations visited by 21st century tourists are mostly monuments to the celebrities of the past. The story of Egypt and its pyramids could not be told without due reference to the pharaohs and their various dynasties. Not only were they revered in life, but their celebrity status continued even after death, and their images can still be seen on temple walls and their lifestyles recreated through other artifacts. In some cases, the remains of their physical bodies survive as objects to be admired and pondered.

Mesopotamia

Our knowledge of the civilizations of ancient Mesopotamia also derives from the stories of its celebrities. Scholars might debate whether there ever was such a person as Gilgamesh, but the epic associated with his name played a formative role in the establishment of the

---

[2] The classic account of celebrity through the centuries is the encyclopaedic work by Leo Braudy, *The Frenzy of Renown: Fame and its History* (New York: Oxford University Press, 1986).

worldview of biblical times, and the various heroes who feature in the story provided the people of the day with a social philosophy as well as personal role models.[3] History in every culture has always consisted of the stories of people. It is personalities who give the past its meaning, and enable us to see its relevance to our own lives.

Ancient Greece

Further to the West, ancient Greek and Roman history would be meaningless apart from the stories of its celebrities, some of whom actively sought publicity in much the same way as today's famous people.

Alexander the Great (356-323 BC) was the founder of what was perhaps the first truly worldwide empire (at least within the geographical parameters then known to him). He was not only a military strategist of some considerable genius, but a self-publicist of the first order. Unlike all his predecessors, and most of his successors, he showed little interest in establishing a dynasty that would

---

[3]   The Gilgamesh epic was an ancient Sumerian story, telling of the historical King of Uruk (somewhere between 2750 and 2500 BC), and including an ancient story of creation. For an accessible version of the text, see: www.ancienttexts.org/library/mesopotamian/gilgamesh/

continue his achievements. Instead, his energy went into promoting his own image, using all the available technologies of the day to ensure that he would be remembered long after he was gone. Coins, sculptures, monuments, palaces—even an entire city (Alexandria in Egypt)—were all carefully crafted to draw attention to himself.

Alexander appointed his own personal 'spin doctor' in the person of Callisthenes, a relative of the philosopher Aristotle, who accompanied him as a war correspondent and personal biographer, and sent regular dispatches back to Greece in instalments, all of them laden with the sort of tittle-tattle that would not be out of place in the tabloid newspapers of the 21st century. It was largely due to these accounts that Alexander came to be hailed as a son of the god Zeus. But like his modern counterparts, Callisthenes fell into the trap of thinking that he himself could make the news as well as reporting it, a mistake that not only led to his dismissal and arrest but eventually to execution as well.

Herod the Great

The Romans continued this tradition, constructing memorials and even whole cities to mark the achievements of their celebrities.

One biblical character who exploited this route to celebrity status was Herod the Great (74-4 BC), ruler of Palestine at the time of Jesus' birth. He was obsessed with his own image, and projected himself as both benefactor and ruthless dictator, rewarding and punishing his friends as well as enemies. He even killed most members of his own family, an action that demonstrated an exceptional degree of cruelty and vindictiveness even by the standards of his day. Yet he was admired for precisely those reasons.

Criminals and terrorists

A similar tradition continues in contemporary celebrity culture, for we seem to admire criminals and terrorists just as much as those whose lives are marked by goodness. Mother Theresa and Hitler were both celebrity icons of the 20th century, and despite the fact that Mother Theresa won the 1979 Nobel Peace Prize, Hitler and his Nazi thugs have arguably enjoyed more widespread and lasting popular acclaim. In spite of the horrendous evil that it represents, the image created by the Nazis, and the mannerisms which accompanied it, have become part of the stock-in-trade of mainline comedians, not to mention the popularity of Nazi uniforms at fancy dress parties. For more than twenty years, the so-called 'great train robber' Ronnie Biggs lived a celebrity lifestyle in South America, and was both admired and envied by the British public even though his only claim to fame was that he was a vicious criminal. In recent years, Osama bin Laden appears to have been elevated to a similar status, and his characteristic clothing also now makes an appearance in fancy dress parties—even, in one infamous episode, at Windsor Castle on the occasion of Prince William's 21st birthday party.

None of this need surprise us—nor should we seize upon such things as evidence of some massive corruption of the culture of 21st century Britain. Most celebrities of the past gained their status not by virtue of their goodness, but because of their notoriety. The celebrities of the American west were individuals who in most other circumstances would have been branded not as heroes, but as criminals. The same is true of many of the notable personalities whose exploits document the history of western expansion and empire-building elsewhere in the world. People were acclaimed because they instilled fear into the hearts of other people, and it seemed to make more sense to esteem them than to oppose them.

Bible Celebrities

The Old Testament

The Bible tells exactly the same story. Indeed, from this perspective a large portion of the Old Testament might be regarded as celebrity stories. This is most obviously true of the narrative books of the so-called Deutero-nomistic History (Joshua–Kings) which recount the exploits of the celebrities of ancient Judah and Israel—but the same thing might also be said of books like Ruth, Daniel and Esther, and maybe some sections of the prophetic books as well. Those rulers whose stories were told at greatest length were often not those who were the most outstanding leaders of their nations, but individuals who became celebrities through some achievement that gave rise to either admiration or fear, or whose private lives were characterized by the sort of salacious behaviour that would not be out of place in magazines like *Hello* and *OK*.

In economic and political terms, Omri (reigned 880-874 BC) was probably the greatest king that the northern kingdom of Israel ever had, yet the Bible says next to nothing about him. His son Ahab, on the other hand (reigned 874-852 BC), achieved far less as a ruler but he deliberately set out to create for himself an image of fame based on notoriety. As a result, his life was recorded in great detail and—like the stories of today's celebrities—was no doubt repeated in many different contexts as both warning and encouragement to others.

The story of King David reflects a similar fascination with the personal lives of celebrities. He is another one whose substantial social and political achievements were noted only briefly, with most of his reign being documented through stories about his personal life, whether as giant killer (1 Samuel 17:19-51), adulterer (2 Samuel 11:2-5), dancer (2 Samuel 6:12-16), or grief-stricken father (2 Samuel 18:31–19:8).

As far back as we can look, there has always been a fascination with the private lives of famous people, especially when they combined both goodness and deviance. In many cases, those same individuals would never have achieved celebrity status at all had they not displayed such moral ambivalence.

The New Testament

The New Testament can also be understood as a series of stories about celebrities. The Gospel writers emphasize that Jesus was acclaimed because he had some distinctive charisma that other religious teachers lacked (Mark 1:22), and as a result thousands of people regularly took time off work just to go and be with him. Moreover, the way in which the evangelists present their accounts of his life utilizes some of the same literary techniques that are so familiar in reports of celebrity lifestyles today. An example would be their descriptions of the 'messianic secret' theme. Who is the real Jesus? Is it the public image, or is there some other hidden dimension to his life that gives access to the authentic person? Does he say the same things to his friends in private as he does in public pronouncements? And do even his closest friends *really* know who he is?[4]

Christians are accustomed to looking at such questions only through historical and theological lenses, but when we examine them in a context of thinking about celebrity culture, it is obvious that the Gospel writers

---

[4] For a typical passage that includes all these themes, see Mark 8:27–9:13, but there are many others.

were exhibiting that same sense of curiosity about the private lives of celebrities that is so common today, among the public as well as among journalists. Even some of the most poignant parts of the story are shot through with this interest in the private lives of famous people—and so we become privy to the inner struggles of Mary as she converses with an angel (Luke 1:26-38), or events in the kitchen at the home of Lazarus and his sisters (Luke 10:38-42), or the private advice that Pontius Pilate received from his wife (Matthew 27:19), and many other similar examples.

It was not long before some of Jesus' disciples, pre-eminently Peter, became celebrities in their own right. Here again, the stories that marked the transition from ordinary individual to celebrity tended to highlight the ambivalence that we still observe today as we delve into the private lives of celebrities to see whether they are consistent with their public image. Peter eventually turned out to be a man of great faith, but in the process, during those first three years of the Lord's ministry, we see him being repeatedly rebuked by Jesus for his lack of spiritual discernment, and then at the very end of his life (according to the 3rd century

Acts of Peter), still being tempted to deny his faith by trying to escape from Rome and certain martyrdom.

This curiosity about individuals who feature in the stories of Jesus' life continued well beyond the first Christian century, giving rise to many pseudo-gospels that claimed to provide otherwise unknown personal details about the various characters who knew Jesus. They still evoke the same fascination today, as evidenced by the reception accorded to Dan Brown's best-selling novel *The DaVinci Code.*[5]

Celebrity, Culture, and Spiritual Values

Despite their diversity, the celebrities of the ancient world all served the same purpose in relation to their various cultures, and the majority of them achieved their celebrity status in the same way. Being a celebrity was based on achievement. Given the nature of the sort of traditional societies in which they flourished, achievement was very often measured in terms of success on the battlefield. Most ancient celebrities were given that status because they accomplished things that were so out of the ordinary and

---

[5] Dan Brown, *The DaVinci Code* (New York: Doubleday, 2003)

beyond the reach of ordinary people that they appeared to be of almost supernatural proportions. It was only a small step from that to the conclusion that the gods must be especially favourable to such individuals.

Of course, only a few people had the opportunity to become celebrities in this way, because not everyone was in a position to be able to lead armies into battle, or otherwise influence the course of history. Only certain classes of people therefore were likely to become famous, and for the most part they did not choose fame for themselves, but rather their destiny was chosen for them.

This is the context in which the social role of the celebrity becomes most transparent, for they most crucially provided role models for the culture. They were more than just high achievers who naturally attracted the admiration of others: they were role models whose exploits embodied the ideals of society, and who therefore became centres around whom their nation could unite and celebrate its distinctive identity and worldview. They embodied the shared values of their people, and the images they projected became the vehicle through which others gained their sense of personal meaning and selfhood.

Most ancient celebrities therefore reflected conventional values and served to reinforce the economic and class systems of the day because their achievements were generally well beyond the reach of ordinary folk. Celebrities were an important symbol of social stability.

Christianity brought different priorities

This is one point at which the Christian story reflected a different set of priorities right from the start. Jesus himself is perhaps the quint-essential example of someone who was not born into a high social position, but who nevertheless accomplished great things that would offer a redemptive role model for others—indeed, that would inspire and empower others to realize the full potential of their own God-given status as people made in the divine image.

This factor alone put a question mark against accepted understandings of celebrity, and opened the door for a different approach to true greatness, exemplified most obviously in the concept of Christian sainthood, which from its inception reflected a different set of priorities than the wider culture.

For one thing, sainthood was accessible to literally anyone, and a majority of those who have been recognized as saints were quite ordinary people. They were not typically individuals who were born to greatness, or who inherited their status through some accident of birth or personal history. Rather, they were people whose great sanctity or devotion had enabled them to break free from the constraints of their social circumstances to accomplish the sort of things that were usually accessible only to those who had been born into favourable circumstances.

Moreover, in order to qualify as a saint, a person needed not only to have displayed exemplary devotion to God, but also to have experienced significant suffering and hardship, often to the point of death. In addition, no-one was recognized as a saint until after their death, which meant that, unlike traditional celebrities, Christian heroes could never parade their status ostentatiously before others.

A pre-Christian notion of 'sainthood'

The notion that saints had a sort of quasi-divine status was rooted in the older traditions of celebrity in the ancient world. It had already been foreshadowed in Jewish circles with Judas Maccabeus' conviction that the dead Onias had special powers to invoke divine aid on behalf of those who were still living (2 Maccabees 15:12ff.; see also 4:33-37).

The same blurring of the distinction between the human and the divine had been found long before in Egyptian culture, where artistic portrayals of the celebrity status of the pharaohs regularly combined the actual likeness of real people with the mythological features of animal deities as a way of emphasizing their distinctiveness.

A similar phenomenon can be observed in the depiction of Greek and Roman celebrities, notably in the epic stories recorded by Homer and others, in which the deeds of national leaders took place in a world populated by the traditional Olympian deities, while conversely the activities of the deities themselves often took place in real places that actually existed and would be known to ordinary citizens. Moreover, whenever celebrities were depicted in works of art they often looked surprisingly similar to the forms in which gods might themselves be characterized.

When placed within the context of the Christian tradition, it is not difficult to draw comparisons between this aspect of ancient celebrity status and the followers of Christ. For Jesus also challenged the distinctions between humanity and divinity, and it was natural to speculate that, if Jesus could take on himself our human status, then maybe the reverse could also be true, and people might partake of the divine nature—especially those who also suffered as a consequence of their faithfulness.

Athanasius expressed the concept in precisely those terms when he wrote of Christ, 'He became man that we might be made God.'[6] This thinking appears to have formed the basis for the belief that saints might have special abilities after death, such as performing miracles of healing or appearing in visions to provide inspiration and courage in times of special need.

Sainthood at its idealistic best

There is no question that it is this combination of humility and greatness that has always given the Christian saints their particular attraction. For on the one hand, they were individuals with whom anyone could easily identify, yet on the other their achievements marked them out as being distinctive and special. Like secular celebrities, they held up a mirror to the culture. But whereas political

---

[6] *On the Incarnation*, 54.3

celebrities reflected the way things were, the saints offered a glimpse of how things might be, and in the process encouraged others to appreciate their own potential and reflect on whom they also might become through spiritual faithfulness.

That, of course, is a description of the notion of sainthood at its idealistic best. For ever since the Reformation, there have been varying assessments of the usefulness of these traditional Christian celebrities. Throughout history, a majority of the world's Christians have found the saints to be a potential source of blessing, and regarded them as symbols pointing to the very nature of God.

Some Protestants, on the other hand (especially from the Reformed and Evangelical traditions), see them as the opposite, as a manifestation of the innate human tendency to substitute the image for the reality, and in the process to downgrade the Creator in favour of the creature. At the same time, though, even conservative Protestants tend to have their own celebrities to whom they look for the same sort of inspiration as has historically been provided by the saints.

Protestant 'saints'

It would be hard to deny that C. S. Lewis occupies that position for large numbers of Christian people today. His elevation to celebrity status has remarkable similarities to the way in which traditional saints were acclaimed. Like many others, the extent of both his piety and his suffering were only recognized after his death. Indeed, he was largely unknown to, and certainly ignored by conservative Protestants during his lifetime, and many of those who were aware of his existence were suspicious of his lifestyle and ideas.

In other circles, Martin Luther King is esteemed as a Protestant 'saint', while some accord similar status to the likes of David Watson or John Wimber. In Scotland, many speak in reverential tones of the memory of Tom Allan, while William Still is widely admired (and followed) as a spiritual role model for Christian ministry.

No doubt those who invoke these and other names would wish to protest that revering someone in this way is not quite the same thing as elevating them to sainthood. But the protest itself highlights one of the intrinsic tensions in any theological understanding of celebrity. And from a missional perspective, Craig Detweiler and Barry Taylor have raised a significant question by noting that 'Protestant skepticism regarding "religious saints" may have encouraged the rampant canonization of secular saints instead.'[7]

The controversial King Saul

One of the most poignant figures of the Hebrew scriptures is Saul, whose elevation to become the first king of Israel has engendered endless discussion among the scholars. In particular, the stories of his anointing have been scrutinized from every conceivable angle in the effort to discern what was really going on. Did Samuel want him to be king, or not? The biblical text seems to answer that both ways: yes, and no. A majority of commentators conclude that the narrative must therefore have been constructed from two originally separate stories, one favouring Saul's appointment (1 Samuel 9:1–10:16: 11:1-15) and the other against it (1 Samuel 8:1-22; 10:17-27).

But what we actually have here is a perfectly coherent internal debate about the

---

[7] Craig Detweiler & Barry Taylor, *A Matrix of Meanings: finding God in pop culture* (Grand Rapids MI: Baker Academic, 2003), p. 117.

nature of celebrity within a biblical worldview. On the one hand, Saul is chosen because he is, or can become, a celebrity by the same definition as that which was generally current in the ancient world: 'to go out before us and fight our battles' (and, of course, to win them, 1 Samuel 8:20). On the other hand, Saul's true celebrity status is ultimately dependent on the extent to which he serves as an authentic reflection of the values of Israelite culture, in which the true measure of celebrity status is not so much personal achievement as faithfulness to the covenant and trust in God.

ॐ

Since celebrities reflect and reinforce the values of their culture, it is only to be expected that different cultures will regard different sorts of actions as worthy of celebrity status, for celebrities reflect in microcosm how different people groups regard themselves. In the earliest Christian centuries, believers drew a contrast between Roman celebrities who were renowned for their military power, and 'heroes of the spirit', whose celebrity status derived from internal qualities rather than external deeds.

Within a biblical frame of reference, there has always been a tension between the commandment not to have any other gods (Exodus 20:3), and the need for some kind of physical embodiment of the ideals of true faith. In this context, celebrities can be good news and bad news at one and the same time. Protestants and Catholics are both right in their estimation of the status of 'saints', because the key question is not so much the individual personality of these celebrities, but the choices made by them, and by those who elevate them to such a position.

Chapter Two

From Fame to Celebrity

In describing the heroes and saints of the past, I have used the word 'celebrity' in order to highlight the continuity between today's celebrity culture and its historical antecedents. But the use of the actual word 'celebrity' is of more recent origin. According to *The Oxford English Dictionary* its first occurrence is in Richard Hooker's work *Of the Laws of Ecclesiastical Polity* (published shortly after his death in 1600), where it refers not to a person but to a place.[1] It seems to have been the mid-19th century before people were described as celebrities, and only in the early 20th century that the word entered into everyday conversation.

In tune with the aspirations of ordinary people

No one can doubt that celebrities wield enormous influence in today's world. In many instances, they have become more influential than our elected representatives. They can also be more in tune with the

---

[1] *Of the Laws of Ecclesiastical Polity*, VII.viii.

aspirations of ordinary people: celebrities like Bob Geldof and Bono have managed to achieve what politicians seemed incapable of doing, by raising moral questions about western lifestyles and worldwide debt.

Spin doctors

The emergence of the professional spin doctor reflects the importance we attach to our celebrities, and the way in which celebrity is no longer automatically defined by reference to social position. Fifty years ago, politicians would have been regarded as celebrities just by virtue of the fact that they were politicians. Today, politicians and other public figures employ spin doctors to turn them into celebrities—with varying degrees of success.

Celebrities have always represented and reflected the prevailing social values, and this shift is all part of the democratization of our society. For various reasons, we no longer trust traditional institutions in the way our forebears would have done, and anyone wishing to be taken seriously has to earn the right to be heard. Politicians are not the only ones in this predicament: the church no longer has an automatic right to speak just because it is the church.

Famous for being famous

There are some other differences between today's celebrities and their equivalents in the past. A recent development is the phenomenon of individuals who become famous just for being famous. The most obvious examples of this are provided by reality TV shows which apparently create overnight celebrities out of people who were previously unknown, and who become famous not because of their accomplishments, but only for being in the public eye. This trend, while real, is vastly overstated and the kind of recognition gained in this way is almost always very short-lived, and may not even be as long as Andy Warhol's fifteen minutes.

Celebrity status based on achievement

It is still overwhelmingly the case that real celebrity status is based on achievement. Bono and Madonna would not be celebrities if they could not sing, nor would David Beckham if he was not a talented footballer. But achievement by itself is no guarantee of fame or public adulation. It never has been: in the ancient world, none of these three would have become celebrities because they lacked the essential qualification of being born into the right families. The extra ingredient that is required today is no longer class-based, but instead is image, appearance, style, behaviour, and personality. Without these qualities, no-one would be regarded as celebrity material. If celebrities act as a mirror, providing role models that reflect the prevailing values of a culture, this need come as no surprise.

An image-based culture

One of the defining characteristics of today's culture is that it is increasingly image-based. A society that values visual images will naturally require and create celebrities with 'image'. So how has this change come about?

Celebrity Style and Cultural Change

1. The traditional society

In the context of this discussion, we can think about Western culture in three broad historical periods. The earliest period might be described as a traditional society, in which the central organizational structures were fixed and unchangeable, and in which bonds of kinship and class provided the underlying foundations. Any given individual understood who they were, and how they related to other people, by reference to their family, their gender, their social class, economic standing, and so on. The boundaries were clearly defined, not least because of the fact that sources of public information were either very sparse or were rigidly controlled by the ruling classes. Most people accepted what they were told, and that included information about who could be regarded as celebrities as well as other matters. Though qualification for inclusion in this élite group invariably required the performance of some extra-ordinary deed, the sort of deeds that were acceptable was carefully defined by the prevailing norms of society.

Mainly élite males

This emphasis on deeds of national significance further limited the group from which celebrities might be chosen, because only those who were born to a certain position ever had the chance to lead armies or rule kingdoms. The same social forces also ensured that most celebrities would be male, and those females who managed to make it were the exceptions rather than the norm. In any case, such women tended to be admired precisely because they did the sort of things that would qualify men for celebrity status (think of Deborah in the Hebrew scriptures, Boudicca in English history, or the French heroine Joan of Arc). There was certainly no possibility that celebrities might be acclaimed on the basis of their looks, not least because most people never got to see them anyway.

Verbal — not visual — reputations

One of the things that often surprises newcomers to the Bible is the complete absence of any descriptions of the physical appearance of its leading characters. But appearance was not important in a traditional society: an ancient hero could be ugly or deformed and still be a celebrity. Moreover, traditional societies were (and still are, in other parts of the world) oral societies, in which news was spread and reputations were made through songs and the telling of epic stories. Because of the limitations of human memory, such songs and stories inevitably focused on the major highlights of a particular individual's accomplishments, rather than recounting their exploits in intimate detail. And for the same reasons, celebrities tended to be few and far between, and were always what Walter Ong calls 'large' or 'heavy' characters.[2]

---

[2]   Walter Ong, *The Presence of the Word* (Minneapolis: University of Minnesota Press, 1981), pp. 204-05.

2. Post-medieval European culture

The invention of printing

The first major move away from this sort of celebrity culture came about in post-medieval Europe, and was made possible by both practical innovation and ideological reflection. The invention of printing changed the way in which stories could be told, for now there was an easier way to record and store large quantities of information about a person's life. Moreover, once it was published in written form, the information was also potentially accessible to anyone (the only limitation being the extent of literacy in any given time and place). Because human memory was no longer the deciding factor in how a story might be told, not only did that mean that more detail could be included, but also that many more stories could be made accessible to greater numbers of people.

Changing cultural boundaries

Alongside this, the Protestant Reformation and subsequent Enlightenment thinking placed a high priority on the individual in his or her uniqueness, and that emphasis itself engendered new ways of understanding personal identity in relation to the norms of the wider culture. By comparison with today's world, there was still a very large number of clearly defined boundaries, but the nature of those boundaries gradually changed, and by the beginning of the 19th century the structures of social cohesion came to be defined in terms of tradition and morality rather than (as previously) class or birthright.

Popular literature and novelists

Moreover, technological developments in printing encouraged the emergence of a whole genre of popular literature, as novelists began to develop new ways of looking at people, based not so much on their external relationships and public deeds, but instead offering extended psychological analysis of their characters replete with detailed descriptions of their private lives and innermost personal thoughts.

Because of their apparently uncanny knack of seeing into people in this way, such novelists themselves became objects of public interest. Unlike the storytellers of oral cultures, who told traditional stories in traditional ways, the new breed of novelists seemed to go beyond official versions of life and its relationships, and spoke openly about human nature in ways that immediately connected with the intimate feelings of their readers.

By the middle of the 19th century the seeds had already been sown for the flowering of stardom and celebrity as we know it today. The technical ability to produce mass circulation newspapers and magazines, and the growing literacy of the population at large, gave more people greater access to this new world of self-awareness. At the very same time, however, the population itself was becoming increasingly urbanized and industrialized, something that separated people from their traditional roots, and therefore from the stories of their own local celebrities who had provided rural communities with their role models and sense of identity.

The invention of the photographic image

Victorian novelist Charles Dickens (1812-1870) enjoyed enormous celebrity during his lifetime, for all the reasons just mentioned. But he was still similar to ancient celebrities in one crucial respect: no-one apart from his close friends knew what he looked like, and he was able to walk the streets of London without anyone recognizing him. Once people were able to see their celebrities, all that changed very rapidly. The invention of the photographic image was the final piece of the jigsaw that bridged the gap between all previous notions of celebrity and the sort of culture we live in today.

3. The 20th century and beyond

To understand the third and final stage in the emergence of modern celebrity we need to cross the Atlantic to the USA, specifically to California, for that is the home of the technological revolution that turned out to be the single most influential factor in the emergence of the sort of celebrity that dominated the 20th century, and with which we are familiar today.

Movies and magazines

The invention of the rotary press, coupled with advanced techniques in photographic reproduction, played a significant part by creating illustrated newspapers and magazines for a burgeoning mass market. But it was the movie industry that changed everything. These developments could have taken place elsewhere in the world without necessarily having the same impact on celebrity culture—and to a limited extent, they did. But when the power of the moving image was combined with the American ideals of democracy and freedom, it created an unstoppable momentum that led directly to the emergence of celebrity culture.

The ideological background to this may be found in the American War of Independence (1775-1783). Its most obvious significance was military and geographic: the former colonies asserted their right to independence from the British crown, and achieved it through armed struggle. But when viewed from the perspective of our discussion here, one of the central elements in the conflict can be seen to be a difference of opinion over what constitutes greatness, and what qualifies an individual to be a celebrity.

The British colonial agents, with their faithfulness to the monarchy, represented a traditional culture in which greatness was determined by kinship, birth and social class. The founders of the American state not only questioned that ideologically, but by their own achievements went on to earn the right to lead their people, and in the process gained their own celebrity status. In the decades that followed, their successors self-consciously modelled the fledgling democracy after the pattern of the city states of ancient Greece, in which celebrities had operated in a sphere that blurred the normal distinctions between gods and humans.

'The American dream'

By the mid-19th century, a similar spiritual emphasis was overtly embraced by some of the leading intellectuals of the day, notably the so-called Transcendentalists (people like Ralph Waldo Emerson, Henry David Thoreau, Margaret Fuller and Bronson Alcott). They, and others like them, helped develop a new national culture emphasizing the freedom of the individual and the utopian aspiration that was to become 'the American dream' in which all citizens would have equal rights and equal opportunities 'under God'. This mystical frame of reference for the culture is represented today by the arcane symbols on the back of a dollar bill: a pyramid, the top of which is depicted as a triangle containing 'the eye of the Great Architect of the Universe'—a common symbol in Freemasonry, which took it over from ancient Egyptian lore in which it was the eye of Horus (Osiris). The inscription surrounding this image declares *annuit coeptis novus ordo seclorum*, 'announcing the birth of a new world order'.

Having ditched the British royal family (celebrities whose claim to fame was based on heritage), they created an alternative meritocracy based on personal achievement. Now, literally anyone could become a celebrity, though still through the traditional routes of innate talent, hard work, and good deeds. By the start of the 20th century, the burgeoning movie industry made that a very achievable prospect, not only for Americans, but also for others like Charlie Chaplin who, if he had stayed in London, would doubtless have spent his entire life trapped in the class into which he was born—but who in Hollywood became a star, in spite of the fact that he was, in traditional British terms, a nobody.

Fact, Fiction and Stardom

The story of celebrity through the ages is really about different ways of telling stories— ranging from the sort of epic stories told orally in the ancient world (and to some extent recorded in its literature), to the more intimate stories recounted by Victorian novelists. But movies created a way of telling stories that was quite different from anything that had gone before. Oral and written stories might well offer graphic descriptions of scenes and personalities, but in the final analysis the mental picture created by the hearer or reader was just that—a mental picture created in the individual imagination.

This was no doubt one reason why Jesus was so fond of telling stories, because it leaves a space for different people to construct their imaginary pictures in ways that naturally connect to their own life experience, which in turn means that a well-told story can challenge different people in different ways.

Movies, however, did not work like that. Though today's directors do indeed craft films that invite different levels of engagement from the audience, the early pioneers had neither the skill nor the knowledge to do so—nor, significantly, did the public have the discernment to perceive the distinction between fact and fiction. Early directors took their role as storytellers very seriously, and the most important thing in their films was the storyline. At first, they never published the names of their actors, believing that the important thing was the characters whom they played on the screen, not who they might be in 'real life'.

Fiction became indistinguishable from facts

But for the audiences, something else was happening: for the first time in history, stories that were intended to be fictional looked indistinguishable from real events. There was a growing fascination with the portrayal of actors doing the sort of things that ordinary people might themselves do in everyday life.[3]

Actors and actresses became 'real'

Moreover, with the development of close-up photography the actors could be seen not just as characters within a bigger picture, but as individuals. Through new camera techniques it became possible to see their facial expressions and gaze into their eyes, apparently giving viewers access to their deepest feelings. It looked as if the actors were no longer playing a part but were just being themselves, and because of this they became 'real' in a way that had never happened with other modes of storytelling. Many of the earliest films had been what today would be called documentaries, depicting actual events, but when close-up

---

[3] For a succinct account of the history of movie-making in relation to celebrity culture, see Samantha Barbas, *Movie Crazy* (New York: Palgrave Macmillan, 2002).

shots became possible, the sight of the actors' faces and expressions convinced viewers that these films could not possibly be fictional narratives, but must be entirely realistic and lifelike—a conclusion that was reinforced by the revelation that some films that were presented as factual were actually nothing of the sort. In some instances it was quite literally the case that 'fiction' seemed more authentic than 'fact'.

Public interest in the actors' off-screen lives

Once actors assumed this new importance, people inevitably wanted to know more about them. They might be bold, courageous, amorous and glamorous on screen—but were they like this in everyday life? And who were they anyway? Carl Laemmle of the Independent Moving Picture Company (IMP) was the first director to release personal details of his actors, and that sparked off an immediate explosion of public interest in their off-screen lives.

The studios soon realized the publicity value of this enthusiasm. Florence Lawrence was an IMP actor, and one of the first to become a celebrity not only through innate talent, but through marketing and promotion. Shortly after her identity became known, the

St Louis Post-Dispatch carried a report of her accidental death, which shocked her admirers —but also turned out to be untrue. Though he never admitted it, this episode was widely believed to be a deliberate publicity stunt on the part of Laemmle. However it came about, he certainly understood the potential of the situation, and to prove that she was still very much alive dispatched her to St Louis, where she was greeted by a large and adoring crowd of the sort which follows celebrities today.

This was not the first time that celebrity status had attracted near-hysterical crowds, though it had more often followed the pattern of traditional sainthood in being accorded to individuals after their death. Previous documented examples of this behaviour would be the funeral of Prince Albert, Queen Victoria's husband and consort, in 1861, or the funeral of British prime minister W. E. Gladstone in 1898. But they were already celebrities by virtue of their social position.

Personal achievement plus effective marketing

Florence Lawrence's reception in St Louis is the first recorded case of such recognition being given to an individual whose celebrity status was not due to innate position, but to personal achievement and (crucially) effective marketing. Within a very short time, the private lives of celebrities became an important part of their public image, and the fictional characters they played on screen began to exercise a growing influence on how they lived the rest of their lives. When Fatty Arbuckle was accused of rape and murder in 1921, his fans were dismayed at the discontinuity between that kind of behaviour and the person they saw on screen, and from then on the studios took deliberate steps to ensure there would not be too much divergence between the public and private images of their stars.

From icons to role models

It was only a matter of time before movie stars were advertising things, and their faces became well known even to people who never went to a cinema. They were living icons of the changes that were then taking place in American society, with the movement of people away from a rural environment into cities, all of it accompanied by a process of rapid industrialization.

In the midst of this social upheaval, the stars became role models for others, for they were the people who seemed to know how to cope in the new environment. Their attitudes and lifestyles addressed a central question of the time, as America shifted from being a production-based society to a consumer culture. Cultural change always creates a demand for new celebrities, because it raises profound questions about identity for all of us.

In the Old Testament, the move from a nomadic to a settled existence created the same sort of vacuum—and Saul was the celebrity figure who would demonstrate to others how to live in the new environment. A generation later, it was David and his successors who would model new ways of being for a dynastic empire. And so on.

In America during the first half of the 20th century, the same questions prevailed: what did it mean to be a person in the new situation? Though the social reasons for it were somewhat different, British and European people were also asking the same question at this period.

Celebrities as 'educators'

Celebrities became educators, showing other people how to live successfully in the new world order. In that respect, their function is still the same. In the 1920s, Mary Pickford was helping women to understand their changing role in society. Today a star like Madonna draws attention to issues such as violence and sexual abuse, and Bob Geldof highlights the need for global cooperation.

How to get yourself noticed in suburbia

Along with increased urbanization and the rise of consumption, other changes were taking place. The traditional values of close-knit rural communities no longer seemed relevant to the new situation. Concern for the family reputation meant nothing in a place where no-one knew anyone else, and it was not a foregone conclusion that the religious beliefs which worked in a traditional culture would fulfil the same purpose in a big city. Later in the 20th century, some movies and TV series would seek to portray the world that had been lost, with programmes such as *Little House on the Prairie* or *The Waltons*—but only as a nostalgic part of a history that everyone knew could never be repeated.

The big question in the impersonal world that was emerging was how to get yourself noticed in a crowded urban situation. The movie stars had the answer to that: it was not through internal values such as honesty, sincerity or integrity, but through external characteristics like friendliness, personal charm and good looks. More than anything else, celebrities had 'personality'. With the appearance of the movie *It* in 1927, the final piece of the jigsaw that became 20th century celebrity culture fell into place, for this film added sexual playfulness to the mix of ingredients that together constituted the ideal image of the sort of person who knew how to cope with the changing culture and its challenge to human identity (and in the process gave rise to a common expression, 'the *It* girl').

On both sides of the Atlantic, the prominence of celebrities as icons of the new culture suited the politicians as well as the advertisers and movie studios, because they served to reassure a sometimes hesitant public that those policies which were having such a dramatic effect on their lives were indeed the right way to enjoy a fulfilling and happy life.

An international influence

Though this form of celebrity was very much a product of American culture, it spread rapidly to other countries because, unlike other mass media (print, radio and TV), movies have always been accessible on a truly international basis. That is still largely the case today, though the rise of the internet and of satellite television may eventually challenge that dominance in the future. In Britain, the Hollywood star system had another hurdle to overcome, because here the route to officially approved celebrity status was still dominated by considerations of class and social position. But that did not stop millions of people going to the cinemas and buying the magazines that would keep them fully informed about the lives of American stars (and the much smaller number of British actors who managed to join them).

From 'flea-pits' to 'picture palaces'

However, it took longer for the British Establishment to appreciate the profound cultural change that had been set in process by the invention of the moving picture. In the earliest years of the movie industry, cinemas were often disparaged as places that respectable people would never visit. There was some justification for this, and the term 'flea-pit' was often not too inaccurate a description. The film companies changed that with the introduction of grand 'picture palaces', and in America audiences of all types flocked to them. But the élite middle-classes in Britain were still reluctant to take them seriously, and as a result found themselves increasingly marginal to the cultural change that was taking place from the middle of the 20th century onwards.

In relation to the church, the arrival of Billy Graham in London in the mid-1950s offers a classic example of this cultural blindness. Taking their cue from the enigmatic American newspaper magnate William Randolph Hearst, who had rocketed the evangelist to celebrity status when he instructed his editors to promote his 1949 Greater Los Angeles Crusade, the British papers highlighted his visit in a way that had never happened for any other religious leader. When Billy Graham arrived by train in central London, the thousands of people who turned out to greet him had already been anticipated by many more who stood by the trackside just to see his train pass as it transported him from Southampton to the capital.

Young, good-looking and oozing charisma

To a country emerging from the hardships of war, and looking for a way to reinvent itself, Billy Graham and his entourage were indeed celebrities. Like the icons of the screen (which by now was the small screen of TV as well as the wide screen of the cinema), they were young and good-looking, oozing image, charisma and 'personality'. It was remarked at the time that the wives of the Graham team wore makeup, jewellery and the sort of clothes that hard-pressed British women could only dream about: even if they had the money, the goods were not in the shops. The people loved them, because they offered a glamorous role model for a culture that needed new direction but had no idea which way to turn. They even attended their meetings, and responded in unprecedented numbers to the invitation to follow Christ.

But the Establishment had no idea how to handle such a situation. Forty years later, the royal family found themselves wrong-footed by the public response to Princess Diana's death, and though they eventually relented it was too little and too late, and the magic of the moment was lost.

The British churches out of touch

Something similar happened with the church and Billy Graham. Innate conservatism and a singular lack of ability to read the signs of the cultural times ensured that he was not wholeheartedly welcomed, and in due course the nation turned to other celebrities to find their role models for the new world that was emerging. Because of their failure to understand popular culture (indeed, a failure to regard pop culture as important at all), the British churches seemed oddly out of touch with the nation's search for new identity and new role models, and no amount of back-peddling in later years could ever rekindle that unique moment of grace. Whether there was a direct cause-and-effect connection is impossible to say, but not long afterwards British Christians found themselves confronted by celebrity role models that would disturb them far more deeply than an American evangelist with brightly coloured ties and a wife who wore earrings.

The influence of Presley and The Beatles

By the mid-1960s, the movie industry was no longer the only source of celebrities. With the emergence of Elvis Presley in the USA, and The Beatles in Britain, a completely different sort of role model came onto the scene. Some of their activities were frowned upon by the guardians of social decency: Elvis with his suggestively gyrating pelvis, and The Beatles with their mop-cut hair styles, which challenged the conventional gender distinctions of the time and, by implication, the distinctive roles of women and men.

Nevertheless for ordinary people, looking for a new image to match the emerging post-war culture, they were all heroes—and, of course, they were soon joined by other musicians who made their own similar, if distinctive, contribution to celebrity culture.

But it was The Beatles and Elvis who turned out to be the archetypes of this new form of celebrity. To an even greater extent than their Hollywood predecessors, they exemplified the way in which celebrity was now detached entirely from considerations of birth or social standing, for they all began life as absolute nobodies—and that was precisely what gave them their mass appeal. They were attractive because of their apparent ordinariness. They had not sought out fame: it came to them almost unannounced. They had the ring of authenticity about them, because in both cases they had a story long before they came to public attention.

Elvis came from a poor family in the Deep South, and started singing as a child in the small Pentecostal church he attended with his parents. In many respects, he was a conventional youth: his songs were based on the musical styles of gospel, together with African American slave music (much of which also had Christian connections), and as a young man he contemplated entering the Christian ministry. As a celebrity, he was not made: he was discovered.

The Beatles were the same. They had played music together when they were still at school, and they did it for their own amusement, as well as for the entertainment of others in the clubs of Hamburg and their native Liverpool.[4] Their hairstyles were also authentic and had nothing to do with their later fame. The one thing that did change was their clothing, and it is well documented how Brian Epstein (their manager) insisted they should wear suits, because he thought that would make them more 'respectable' than wearing leather jackets. Everything about them both reflected and created the cultural mood of the 1960s: their known humble origins, plus their conservative dress, reassured the public that they were nice boys who could be trusted, while their gender-bending hairstyles reflected the fact that they were not unaware of the major themes of the day, in which experimentation with sexuality was to play a major role. Their nickname, 'the Fab Four', summed them up accurately: as

---

[4] See Ian Inglis (ed.), *The Beatles, Popular Music, and Society* (London: Macmillan, 2000).

well as being 'fabulous' in terms of their abilities, their identity was also 'fabricated' in the way they were presented to the public.

When they later made a couple of films, their role as iconic models for personal identity in the emerging culture was confirmed. In *A Hard Day's Night* and *Help!* they were not actors, but played themselves. In doing so they revealed, in an ostensibly fictional setting, the truth of who they 'really' were as they strove to cope with the personality-driven media image of them.

The Tabloids and reality TV shows

The more usual medium through which people get to know about the private lives of their celebrities is through the tabloid press—or, increasingly nowadays, through reality TV shows such as *Celebrity Big Brother*. By revealing their inner selves, celebrities both reflect the prevailing concerns of the culture (for they are themselves a part of it), while at the same time playing up to the image which is generated around them, as role models for the culture. The Beatles certainly did both, and when in 'real life' they went off to India to search for spiritual meaning, people recognized their searching as an authentic reflection of the cultural anxiety that was then gripping Western culture, and followed them in droves.

Post-modern Celebrity

The immediate post-war generation, whose teenage years were the 1960s, lived on the cusp of a revolution whose full effect is still being worked out, but which will almost certainly turn out to have been as great a paradigm shift as the changes that took place with the invention of writing, or the discovery that the earth is not flat but a globe. The shorthand way of referring to this is to speak of a move from modernity to post-modernity. There is a good deal of debate about the nature of this change, and over the precise meaning of terms like 'post-modernity' and 'postmodernism' (with or without the hyphen).

This is not the place for that discussion, except to note that I am simply using the term 'post-modernity' here as a shorthand way of referring to 'whatever it is that is going on in western culture today'—and always with a hyphen, to indicate that it is more defined by what it is not, than what it is. It is post-modern, in the sense of coming after (and questioning, though not necessarily rejecting) the values of modernity, by which I mean the culture rooted in recent European history (the so-called 'Enlightenment'—another disputed term), but behind which lies the rationalist-materialist worldview of ancient Greece and Rome. But, however we describe or define it, it is obvious that today's world is radically different from what it was thirty or forty years ago.

'I don't know who I am'

One of the indisputable characteristics of post-modernity is an uncertainty over who we actually are. I remember being in Hollywood for a gathering of movie directors, theologians, and storytellers, at which we were discussing the question of spirituality and identity as it is being presented in today's films. There were about thirty of us, including a small number of young people who had been specially invited from within the gang culture of Los Angeles.

After much pretentious conversation among the *cognoscenti*, someone asked these young people how our concerns might relate to their situation. A young woman stood up and, pointing to the various pieces of clothing she was wearing, said, 'Just look at me. I don't know who I am. My identity is defined not by any inner qualities, but by the labels of the clothes that I wear—which means, the clothes that advertisers persuade me I need to have in order to be trendy or cool.'

She went on to castigate the media people who were present, and told them that the best contribution they could make would be to stop what they were doing, because the sort of films they were making 'have robbed my generation of all meaningful role models' and this was why identity was a matter of choice, dictated by the goods that were available, in this case clothing.

It was not what any of us wanted to hear, but she was right. Post-modern theorists have suggested that identity itself is an illusion, and we can all become who we want to be. Identity has become 'a matter of choice, style, and behavior rather than intrinsic moral or psychological qualities ... identity is a game that one plays, that one can easily shift from one identity to another'.[5] The search for identity is consequently more intense and far-reaching today than at any period in recent history.

Think of the rise of tribalism throughout Europe, expressed not just in traditional

---

[5]   Douglas Kellner, *Media Culture* (London: Routledge, 1995), p. 242.

nationalistic terms, but through people identifying with, or creating, new configurations of community (men's movements, women's movements, the gay community, the green movement, and so on).

Failing to engage with deeper questions

The ubiquitous fascination with gender is part of this, for sexual experimentation is one of the most obvious ways to explore who you might really be. The fact that this has more to do with identity than it does with sex *per se* also goes a long way towards explaining why the church's concerns are mystifying to most ordinary people, because Christians tend to be bothered about who has sex with whom, and how they do it, rather than engaging with the deeper questions of purpose and meaning that lie beneath the surface.

The same search for identity is reflected in other aspects of life as well. In the world of employment, for example, a diminishing number of people operate with clearly defined roles, and significant numbers work in the field of information technology, where the production and manipulation of images is central to what they do. So why not manipulate the self, and see what happens?

Hyping it to make it happen

I remember an advertising expert once advising me that 'if you hype a thing enough, you can make it happen'. He was right, and the event we were discussing (a Christian celebration) did indeed take place in spectacular fashion, largely because I took his advice.

This is the context in which reality TV programmes operate. To a society uncertain of its corporate identity, and to individuals searching for a new identity, they create a platform on which many different ways of being can be tried out. The TV provides the tools with which to create a personality, which is why otherwise ordinary people apply in their thousands to get into programmes such as *Big Brother* or *Pop Idol*, and dysfunctional families queue up to air their problems on *The Jerry Springer Show*, or its many imitators.

If their stories and alleged talents seem bizarre and unbelievable, then there is plenty of evidence to suggest that in some instances this is indeed the case, and people use these opportunities to experiment with who they might become, rather than necessarily projecting an image of who they actually are or believe themselves to be.

Because so many of us lack confidence about our own true identity and life purpose, we tune in to these programmes, hoping that we can learn something about how we also might be transformed into 'cool' individuals, with all the trappings of the celebrity lifestyle that appear to go with the image.

☙

There have been many changes and adaptations in the story of celebrity from ancient times to the 21st century, but this one central core still remains. Celebrities not only reflect the prevailing values of any culture, but they also simultaneously provide the inspiration for new ways of being. In that sense, we all get the celebrities that we deserve.

Chapter Three

God and the Cult of Celebrity

I have deliberately included the word 'cult' in the chapter heading here, because there is a surprising overlap between the ways we speak of celebrities and the language of traditional religious terminology. Not only do we talk about 'image', but celebrities are sometimes referred to as 'idols'—both of them words that are used of false deities in the Bible. Even the word 'stars' makes a subtle connection with the religious beliefs of ancient Greece and Rome, in which traditional deities were also identified with heavenly bodies.

The apparent similarities do not end there, and recent years have seen a growing awareness of the way in which celebrities function as spiritual leaders. Anthropologists as well as theologians[1] now regularly talk of

---

[1] See, for example, Christopher H. Evans & William R. Herzog, *The Faith of 50 Million: baseball, religion, and American culture* (Louisville: Westminster John Knox Press, 2002); Michael Grimshaw, 'I can't believe my eyes: the religious aesthetics of sport as postmodern salvific moments', in *Implicit Religion* 3/2 (2000), pp. 87-99; Shirl J. Hoffman, *Sport and Religion* (Champaign, IL: Human Kinetics Books, 1992); Daniel Miller, Peter Jackson, Nigel

pop concerts, sports events, and even shopping, as spiritual experiences, and study the symbolism of their 'temples' in the effort to understand the significance of the rituals that are regularly enacted there. Spin doctors and publicists frequently operate like a priestly caste for their idols, exposing them to the public while at the same time keeping them at a distance so as to retain control of the fans ('worshippers'). There are often links between idols and sex and power, and like the religious idols of old, celebrities can provide an identity for disparate groups, who might then find themselves locked in conflict with the followers of different celebrities.

Craig Detweiler and Barry Taylor identify considerable theological meaning in this aspect of celebrity culture, suggesting that the way we create, worship and then often destroy our idols is a sort of secular reflection of the redemptive rituals of traditional sacrifice: 'Like Old Testament scapegoats,

---

Thrift, Beverley Holbrook, and Michael Rowlands, *Shopping, Place and Identity* (New York: Routledge, 1998); George Ritzer (ed.), *McDonaldization: the Reader* (Thousand Oaks: Pine Forge Press, 2002); Ira G. Zepp, *The New Religious Image of Urban America: the shopping mall as ceremonial center* (Niwot: University Press of Colorado, 1997, 2nd ed.).

celebrities bear the community's weaknesses. Having risen to great heights, they often end up cast out for our collective sins.... they experience almost every sacrament, from the baptism of fame to enforced public confessions to the absolution of sins.... Stars travel a well-paid road from idol to scapegoat. ... [reminding] us how fleeting fame is, how foolish our efforts top generate immortality... washed-up stars... serve as human sacrifices, carrying our culture's many sins—especially our misplaced faith in celebrities.'[2]

A vicarious role on behalf of the community

TV programmes like *Big Brother* follow this ritualistic pattern very closely, though Princess Diana is probably the most outstanding example of a celebrity playing such a vicarious role on behalf of the community; it is not difficult to trace more or less exact parallels between traditional Christian understandings of the life and death of Jesus, and the way that she was perceived by the popular imagination.[3]

---

[2] Craig Detweiler & Barry Taylor, *A Matrix of Meanings: Finding God in Pop Culture* (Grand Rapids: Baker Academic, 2003), pp. 111-13.

[3] See John Drane, *Cultural Change and Biblical Faith* (Carlisle: Paternoster, 2000), pp. 78-103.

Culture and Contextualization

A fantastic opportunity for the gospel

In the light of all this, I have spent a good deal of time reflecting on one central question: *Does today's celebrity culture make it easier, or more difficult, to witness to the values of the gospel?* My conclusion is that our fascination with celebrity, and the post-modern search for meaning which has engendered it, offers a fantastic opportunity for the gospel if we are prepared to step outside some of our traditional boxes, and really get to grips with working out how the Christian message can be contextualized in today's world.

The culture in which we now operate has its own language and thought forms, which are quite different from the ways in which we have traditionally articulated Christian belief. For generations we have trained people to go as missionaries to other countries by insisting they learn the appropriate local language and understand the culture before they can have any chance of sharing the gospel in a way that will enable its challenge to be heard.

Learning many cultural languages

If we are to be effective in Western culture today, we need to recognize the importance of learning the cultural language in which people express their search for meaning and purpose, which is ultimately a search for God. Actually, we might need to learn many different cultural languages, for the way a teenager might express his or her spiritual search is likely to be quite different from what we will find among people in their fifties and sixties (brought up in the 1960s), while the terms in which older people are able to speak of God will be different again.

In relation to effective mission, though, the most important distinction for us to recognize is that between popular culture and intellectual high culture. It is generally the case that Christians feel more at home in high culture than in popular culture. In the past, that provided a highly significant forum for contextualization of the gospel, because the educated classes were also generally the ruling classes, and they were the ones who laid down social norms. Today, things are rather different, not just because of the influence of the entertainment culture but also as a result of the rise of the internet. Literally anyone can share their ideas with the whole world through websites, blogs, bulletin boards, and so on, and be taken seriously—and make a difference.

'The top' has gone forever

The day when big ideas only filtered down from the top is gone forever, and our fascination with celebrities is a manifestation of that. Indeed, as we have noticed in the previous chapter, 'the top' no longer exists in any recognizably traditional form. This is itself an interesting reflection of a major characteristic of the Kingdom of God, in which the first are last, and vice versa (Matthew 19:30), and the surprising correlation between the two should encourage us to reflect more deeply on the nature of post-modernity in relation to the gospel.

Has the concept of truth gone?

What exactly are the values of today's culture which are both reflected and modelled by our celebrities? Philosopher François Lyotard writes about our alleged 'incredulity toward metanarratives'[4] while Christian apologist Douglas Groothuis confidently claims that 'The concept of truth as absolute, objective and universal has gone ... Ultimately, truth is

---

[4] François Lyotard, *The Postmodern Condition* (Minneapolis: University of Minnesota Press, 1993), p. *xxiv*.

what we make it to be.'[5] It can certainly seem like that if we only ever listen to the privileged voices of academics.

However, social scientist Peter Berger puts their opinions in context with his observation that 'When intellectuals travel, they usually touch down in intellectual circles—that is, among people much like themselves. They can easily fall into the misconception that these people reflect the overall visited society, which of course is a big mistake.' He goes on to speculate how secular Western academics might react when faced with the sort of traffic gridlock that is created by people going to church on Sunday mornings in Texas: 'What happens then is a severe jolt of what anthropologists call culture shock.'[6]

Historic failures of the church

As I listen to the voices of ordinary people, I have concluded that most Christian apologists have allowed themselves to be led into the same sort of cultural blind alley by listening too attentively to the philosophers of the

---

[5] Douglas Groothuis, *Truth Decay* (Downers Grove: InterVarsity, 2000); quotation is on the cover.

[6] Peter Berger, *The Desecularization of the World* (Washington DC: Ethics & Public Policy Center, 1999), p. 11.

postmodern,[7] and not paying sufficient attention to the cadences of popular culture. This is not the first time that we have made that mistake. I have already highlighted the way in which the church's ambivalence about Billy Graham failed to understand the popular mood of the 1950s. But I could also mention the inordinate amount of energy expended by theologians in the 1920s and 1930s on matters like 'demythologizing' the gospel, because they had convinced themselves that nobody any longer believed in the supernatural—yet at the very same time, huge numbers of ordinary people were falling over themselves to consult psychic mediums in the effort to connect with loved-ones who had been lost in World War 1.

A similar pattern repeated itself in the 1960s, with theological debate dominated by arguments about things like 'the death of God', while everyone else was following The Beatles, who not only took it for granted that God was very much alive but were actively searching for that transcendent connection that might give new meaning and purpose to

---

[7] For detailed arguments as to why I question these ideas, see most recently John Drane, 'Post-modernity, Truth, and the Rise of the Documentary', in *Theology Notes and News* 52/2 (2005), pp. 16-21.

life. We are in danger of making the same mistake again by taking intellectuals and academics too seriously, and ignoring the cries of ordinary people. For an incarnational faith to do so is surely a contradiction in terms: if incarnation means anything in this context, it must involve as a minimum that we take people seriously.

So what are people wrestling with today? On metanarratives ('big stories'), I see no evidence to suggest that we no longer believe in them, only that we have rejected damaging metanarratives from the past and that we are now searching for new ones to take us safely forward into the future. Nor do I believe that people have rejected the idea of truth, but rather that they want to explore it for themselves instead of having it handed down to them in a disembodied way by experts who think they know best.

The basis of real truth is relational and personal

Experience has now demonstrated what an older biblical wisdom knew all along: that truth as abstract propositions can never address the central existential questions of everyday life, and that real truth—wherever it may be found—will have a basis in what is relational and personal, because it is in relationships that we encounter the things that are of most ultimate importance in life.

One thing we all struggle with is the rapid and universal change in almost every area of existence. If even our most immediate forebears were to come back to life, they would encounter today's world as an alien place in a way that would not have been the case for virtually any previous generation —certainly not for any in the last five hundred years or so. The rate of change accelerates all the time, and there is virtually nothing we can now do in the same way our grandparents did it—not even everyday tasks such as buying or cooking food.

Those institutions which attempt to stick to old ways either fail to survive, or struggle to reinvent themselves, something that is as true of the church as it is of the systems of politics, education and world economics. Added to this is the further factor that we all have much wider horizons than previous generations. In the past, few people had any real knowledge of other cultures because the only way of gaining it was by travelling to different parts of the world, which was simply not possible for the majority. Today, not only can we all travel more easily and cheaply, but the world comes right into our own homes through the medium of TV. As a consequence we all know that the old Western traditions, with which we are increasingly dissatisfied, are in any case not the only way of doing things and of living a good life. In this situation, it is natural to experiment with different styles that might be drawn from multiple world contexts. When we throw into this mix the deep sense of disillusionment, despair and anxiety felt by many people, we have the cultural matrix which both produces today's celebrities and also holds them up as icons of people who are addressing these questions.

More than ten years ago, sociologist George Ritzer traced much of our personal anxiety to the fact that

> Human beings, equipped with a wide array of skills and abilities, are asked to perform a limited number of highly simplified tasks over and over ... forced to deny their humanity and act in a robot-like manner.[8]

Novelist Douglas Coupland[9] eloquently expresses how that manifests itself in everyday life:

---

[8] George Ritzer, *The McDonaldization of Society* (Thousand Oaks CA: Pine Forge Press, 1993), p. 26.

[9] Douglas Coupland, *Microserfs* (London: Flamingo, 1995), p. 313.

people without lives like to hang out with other people who don't have lives. Thus they form lives.

And most recently, Astronomer Royal Martin Rees has named what many people fear the most:

> I think the odds are no better than fifty-fifty that our present civilisation on Earth will survive to the end of the present century ... What happens here on Earth, in this century, could conceivably make the difference between a near eternity filled with ever more complex and subtle forms of life and one filled with nothing but base matter.[10]

Key contemporary concerns of popular culture

For me, these three quotations eloquently define the key underlying concerns of today's popular culture: a rejection of damaging metanarratives from the past, combined with uncertainty about who we are (especially in relationship to others), and all of it overlaid with a growing sense of fear and foreboding as to what the future might hold—always supposing that we can with any confidence expect there to be much of a future.

---

[10] Martin Rees, *Our Final Century* (London: Heinemann, 2003), p. 8.

These are the things that people are struggling with, and which shape our expectations of celebrities. Because we feel we have been betrayed by the metanarratives of the past, all we have left is experimentation to try and identify the source of a truth that can be trusted. And because our trust in institutions claiming to have the truth has so often been abused and betrayed, we feel we have no options but to look within ourselves as we search for the meaning of life. Just as the early movie stars showed audiences how they might live in the change from a rural to an industrialized urban culture, so today's celebrities are engaged in showing how we might survive this even bigger change from the certainties of modernity to the cultural flux that we describe as post-modern.

Finding God at Work

What can we make of all this theologically? Where does God fit in? This question could easily take us well beyond our immediate concerns here, not to mention the intended length of this book, and I must therefore be selective in my comments.

No cultural no-go areas for God

When we survey the history of Christian faith, it is clear that the gospel has never been a set of abstractions that can be expressed independently of the cultural matrix of particular times and places. So the most important issue is not about whether this or that aspect of today's culture may or may not be compatible with the gospel—but about how the gospel might be appropriately expressed within the culture. It is not therefore appropriate to talk of making the gospel relevant, still less about advocating ways of making it trendy. We ought rather to be asking how the message can be incarnated within the culture.

Theologically, this way of articulating the challenge stems from the notion of the *missio Dei* (that this is God's world, and God is therefore at work in it), which requires us to ask not, Where does God fit in? but, How is it possible that God would not be at work here? For if God is God, Creator and Sustainer of this world (not to mention loving Redeemer and a host of other things), then there can in principle be no cultural no-go areas where God is by definition either powerless or excluded. And that must include celebrity culture.[11]

Celebrity culture and Christian tradition

When we reflect on it from that angle, there are indeed some surprising correlations between what is going on in celebrity culture and what we otherwise know of the revealed character of God within the Christian tradition. For example, we have already noted that a major difference between today's celebrities and those of past generations is that now literally anyone can be a celebrity, because fame no longer depends on accidents of birth or opportunity, but is potentially open to all.

Moreover, as we noted when discussing the rise of movie stars, being ('personality') is now on an equal footing with doing (noble deeds, bravery in battle, or whatever). In both these respects, today's definition of celebrity has a much closer affinity with some key

---

[11]   Readers will recognize that this is a totally different approach to gospel and culture matters than that promoted by Richard Niebuhr, *Christ and Culture* (New York: Harper & Row, 1951), and which has set the terms of reference for the discussion for the last fifty years and more. For further reflection on this, I will have to point to my forthcoming book *After McDonaldization: how not to do Church* (London: Darton Longman & Todd, 2006).

biblical notions than was the case with older notions of what might constitute fame. The very first page of the Bible sets out the foundational principle that people are of value not because of their accomplishments, but simply by virtue of being made 'in the image of God' (Genesis 1:26-27), without any reference to social class, military achievement, gender, or any other marks of greatness that have been elevated over the centuries. One might go further and suggest that the many tensions reflected in the Old Testament about the nature of true fame are eventually resolved in favour of the view that greatness does not stem from dynastic succession or military prowess, but from the interior worth of the human spirit when in tune with the will of God.

This same point is further emphasized in the teaching of Jesus, who repeatedly insisted that it is not through personal achievement that individuals commend themselves to God, but rather through the intrinsic worth endowed on every person through being made in the divine image, and therefore dependent on God for whatever recognition may come their way.

This angle was, of course, then repeated and reinforced by St Paul with his contrast between law and grace. Theologically, one might describe the traditional criteria for celebrity as a manifestation of salvation-by-works (doing things), while today's emphasis on personality is much closer to a biblical picture of grace (where being is primary). There is of course one difference, namely that biblical grace is about being before God.

Elvis Presley

When we look at the role models offered by specific celebrities, there are many other intimations that God is far from absent from this scene. Elvis Presley and Madonna are two of the most enduring celebrities, and in Elvis's case his popularity has extended well beyond his lifetime in such a way that he has been accorded some of the attributes of traditional sainthood. His background in Pentecostal churches has already been noted, and Christians often assume that he abandoned that when he became a celebrity.

The reality was rather different, and it is well documented that he read his Bible and prayed regularly and was not only eager to converse about spiritual matters but very knowledgeable in doing so. In the mid-1960s he became a movie star as well as a singer, and during the time that he lived in southern

California he held regular Bible studies at his Bel Air home. In the 1970s, he regularly included Christian music in his concerts, most notably the hymn *How Great Thou Art*, which entered the musical mainstream as a result. He also on occasion read passages from the Bible on stage during his concerts, and on one famous occasion when a fan shouted from the audience, 'Elvis, you're the King', he responded with, 'No honey, there is only one King and that is Jesus Christ.' Of course, he was not perfect, but the very ambivalence of a person who could be good and bad at the same time is an important aspect of celebrity in a time of cultural change.

Madonna

Madonna has been at the top of her profession for more than twenty years now, and has enjoyed celebrity status throughout that time. She is another one who embodies all the characteristics of celebrity in a post-modern culture, and her career demonstrates very clearly how celebrity runs parallel with the search for identity in today's world. Moreover, she is a very sophisticated performer who is well aware of the role that she plays in helping people find a new identity, and everything she does is carefully crafted in full awareness of its wider cultural significance.

Postmodern ideologues might argue that nothing any longer has meaning today, but Madonna's concerts and music videos stand in sharp contradiction to that opinion, with their intricately constructed scenarios that can be accessed and understood on any number of different levels by different audiences. As a result, she is not only admired by her fans, but studied by scholars who have come to regard her work as a microcosm of the culture. Like Elvis, she has also at times been severely criticized by Christians, which makes her an especially useful example for our purposes.

Right from the start of her career in the 1980s, Madonna has both mirrored and encapsulated all the elements in the post-modern search for identity and purpose. Who exactly is she? She has in turn been dancer, musician, model, singer, movie star, stage actress, businesswoman, spiritual seeker, wife and mother, author and storyteller.

In exploring these different identities, she has been (in cultural terms) both radical and conservative. She has freely used images of sexuality to explore new identities, mostly by pushing the boundaries of conventional heterosexual behaviour, but also famously French-kissing Britney Spears on stage in a way calculated to raise questions of sexual orientation and gender-bending. At the same time, she has used fashion in highly sophisticated ways as a means of creating and recreating new identities, and in the process affirming the norms of a consumer society, in which one can construct a new self not through lifestyle experimentation but by being conformist and going to the shops.

In the past, a person's clothes and general appearance denoted social class, and therefore identity. In the Middle Ages, there were even rules about which class could wear which clothes. But by the early 19th century, traditional dress codes started to disappear and in principle anyone could wear anything. The cost frequently served as a control mechanism, but even in the early 20th century when fashion was readily available to anyone there were still unspoken expectations about who would wear what sort of clothing. But as part of the sixties revolution, clothing came to play an increasing role in the emergence of a new sense of identity.

Madonna embodies this, by demonstrating the range of new identities that clothing makes possible. When reading stories from her children's story books, she might dress like Snow White; but she can also appear on stage with outfits that incorporate unexpected items such as rosaries and crucifixes, which in the past would never have been associated with anything other than organized religion.

Madonna's role in raising key questions

Madonna's intellectual sophistication is not a recent development. Her music video *Express Yourself*, for example, produced in 1989, was a highly complex exploration of the issues of the day, notably social class, sexuality and gender in which she made conscious use of Fritz Lang's classic film *Metropolis* (produced in 1927, but set in time around the year 2000). In it, Lang depicted a futuristic city constructed on an industrial base, which appeared to have delivered a near-Utopian lifestyle to its inhabitants who lived in palatial apartments made of glass and concrete. Under the surface, though, the luxurious lifestyle of the masters turned out to be supported by an army of subhuman slaves toiling away for a pittance. In the end, the workers revolted and destroyed the system that had enslaved them.

Influenced by the humanistic assumptions of 1920s Germany, Lang had presented a scenario in which all such conflicts would eventually be resolved with justice and fairness, but Madonna used these images in a completely different way, challenging that worldview by instead depicting a world in which the tensions generated by the struggle to be fully human are actually an intrinsic aspect of our existence. Not only did she expose the bland liberalism of a worldview that is now discredited, but the way she did it raised questions that connect with some strong biblical themes, most obviously the struggle depicted in Adam and Eve's life after the Fall, the many debates in the Wisdom literature and some of the Psalms regarding the moral nature of the universe and the apparent futility of life, not to mention the personal dilemmas described so eloquently by St Paul in Romans 7. In the process of doing this, she also raised the sort of questions that invite an eschatological response.

Madonna's reverence for Christian values

Madonna does more than raise questions. She also offers answers, and those answers can also reflect Christian values in very positive ways. For example, in the video of *Papa Don't Preach* she appeared as a blonde teenager who got pregnant and was seeking advice from her father—but who made it clear from the start that she was not going to have an abortion.

At the time, Madonna denied that she was intending to take sides in the abortion debate, but her own career as a mother has subsequently demonstrated a very traditional approach both to having children and raising them, and her insistence on being a hands-on parent is matched by the extensive arrangements that are made so she can be with them even while on tour.

Another example of Madonna's reverence for traditional Christian values can be found in *Like a Prayer*, where she compares and contrasts 'images of an inside and outside world, where the outside is the site of racial and sexual violence, bigotry and injustice. The inside world of the church, however, is one of love, community, and goodness....'[12] More recently, she has openly presented herself not only as wife and mother, but also as a serious spiritual searcher questioning the underlying materialistic values of the culture.

---

[12] Douglas Kellner, *Media Culture* (London: Routledge, 1995), p. 277.

Getting in step with God

The point of drawing attention to Elvis and Madonna is not to offer any sort of apologetic for them personally, but simply to point out that celebrity culture is by no means as anti-Christian as some people imagine. Nor are these two isolated examples: the point could have been made just as easily by reviewing the celebrity status of David Beckham, or the music group 'Faithless', among others.[13] In order to share the gospel effectively, we need not only to read the signs of the times, but also to be open to seeing where God might already be at work within the culture. Authentic mission is then not a matter of Christians doing work on God's behalf, but of taking intentional steps to get alongside what God is already doing, in a process that is itself a witness to the priority of grace.

Mission and Ministry in Celebrity Culture

Practical observations about Christian ministry in today's world have been interwoven throughout the discussion so far,

---

[13] For more along these lines, see John Drane, 'Contemporary culture and the reinvention of sacramental spirituality' in Geoffrey Rowell & Christine Hall (eds), *The Gestures of God: Explorations in Sacramentality* (London: Continuum, 2004), pp. 37-55.

but it will be worthwhile drawing to a conclusion by highlighting some specific practical matters that should concern us as Christians in a celebrity culture. The point has repeatedly been made that celebrities reflect the underlying values and concerns of any culture. There can be no doubt that today we are concerned about big questions of meaning, identity and purpose. We literally do not know who we are and what we are for. What can Christians bring into this situation?

1. Human worth and fallen human nature

First of all must be a sense of the worth and value of human persons. Christians are widely perceived as judgmental, quick to speak in condemnation of others but having little else to say. A hundred years ago, our forebears were not facing the same identity crisis as we face today. On the contrary, they had a good self-image. They literally ruled the world, and considered themselves to be invincible. In that situation, it was appropriate for Christians to draw attention to the fact that people were not as good as they thought they were, and that good works are not the ultimate pathway to spiritual meaning.

Today, we struggle with the opposite. As individuals and as a nation we have a very poor self-image, knowing what previous generations accomplished in the past, but doubting our own ability to shape the future. This self-understanding is widely held among our young people, and is at the root of the alarming increase in the level of self-harm and suicide, as well as contributing to the culture of binge drinking and drugs (both of which not only dull the pain of not knowing who you are, but are used by some as potential routes to transcendence).

In this situation, telling people how lost they are is likely to reinforce the values of the culture, rather than challenging them. To be truly radical (and appropriately biblical), we should be insisting that actually we are all individuals of enormous value and worth because we are 'made in God's image', and our very embodiment has been blessed by the fact that the Son of God has shared in it.

Using terms like 'creation' and 'incarnation' may not be the best way to communicate these truths, but the reality they represent is what our culture desperately needs to hear, and welcomes when it does in terms that it can comprehend. Jesus is said to have looked on those who were lost, and had compassion on them (Matthew 9:36). We need to learn from him.

As part of this, we may also need to do some serious reflection on the nature of sin. In the days of the empire, our forebears did indeed think they were perfect, and it was appropriate to have their shortcomings pointed out to them. No-one today needs to be told that they are sinners. They may not use that actual terminology, and might instead talk of their lives being in a mess, or their relationships being fractured and unhealthy, but the reality is the same.

Moreover, many people find themselves in such circumstances through no fault of their own—not so much because they are sinners, but because they are sinned against. We have always known that sin is more than just things that people do, but today we need to take more seriously the communal—indeed the global and cosmic—nature of the fallenness that afflicts all things, and which is at the heart of a biblical understanding of sin, and consequently of salvation also.

2. Honesty and integrity in discipleship

Alongside this, I wonder if we need also to learn to live more comfortably within the ambivalence of our own experience. I regularly meet people who are incapable of taking Christians seriously because, they say, we are all 'hypocrites'. By using that term, they do not usually mean to suggest that we are self-consciously devious or dishonest. On the contrary, there is an enormous amount of respect for what Christians have accomplished in the world, and the good things we continue to do. But one thing that people today cannot tolerate is a lack of integrity. If we share the same struggles as everyone else—in relationships, tough decisions, sexuality, internal motivation, and so on—why do we so often present a public face that sends out a different message?

This kind of questioning is related to the fact that we no longer like our celebrities to be completely perfect. In fact, we would not believe them to be credible as people if they were, or seemed to be. Life today just seems to be too tough and complex for anyone to rise above it all and come up with the perfect solution to every problem. The idea that someone else might know all the answers would not only depress us further, but would be simply unbelievable.

On the other hand, the knowledge that an individual can live through the pain while still struggling to be a person of value is likely to be good news. This is precisely why Princess Diana became such an icon for a whole generation: even though she was rich and well connected in a way that few others ever could be, she became an inspiration for millions of ordinary people, because she evidently had the same struggles as them in her own life.

But the same phenomenon is there in the Bible, many of whose celebrities exemplified exactly the same sense of moral and spiritual ambivalence: this was true of virtually all the Old Testament heroes, but was also the case for the disciples (especially Peter) as well as Paul. The sort of honest discipleship we find there is so attractive precisely because it reflects the reality of the struggle that resonates within every human heart.

3. Openness about personal spirituality

Another matter not unconnected with this is the way that some Christians find it really difficult to talk openly about their personal spirituality. For more than ten years now I have had an active engagement as a Christian with people who are attracted by other spiritual pathways. They talk openly about what they have discovered, and describe personal experiences of a spiritual nature in a completely unselfconscious way and often in great detail. They simply cannot comprehend Christians who prefer to keep their inner spiritual lives under wraps, as something private and not to be spoken about.

In a world of reality TV, where people go on shows like *Jerry Springer* with the express intention of revealing all there is to know about them, or where they live for ten weeks in the goldfish bowl that is *Big Brother*, open to view 24/7, we will need to learn to speak with greater openness about God, otherwise many people will simply conclude that if we have little or nothing to say, that is because we have no meaningful spiritual experience of which to speak.

Christians in general seem to find it much easier to speak about rules, about personal morality, and about abstruse belief systems, than they do of transcendence, and this reticence has contributed to the creation of a situation in which the church no longer occupies the spiritual high ground in our culture.

4. Jesus has become the unknown god

It is easy to be critical of the way in which people model themselves on what they see celebrities doing, but because of a reluctance among Christians to engage with the cultural language within which people today speak of their search for spiritual reality, the gospel goes unheard more or less by default.[14] Very many people are totally unaware of the existence of any options other than those presented to them through the media, which of course means celebrities.

At the same time, we are increasingly dissatisfied with trying to find meaning solely through external image, and there are significant moves to reintroduce ideals into public discourse, most notably through the endeavours of people like Bob Geldof and Bono, who are themselves celebrities.

Running parallel with that, however, is enormous ignorance of the one story that Christians believe offers the greatest ideal of all, namely the story of Jesus. In Britain today, that story is completely unknown to most people under forty, and a fair number who are older than that.

---

[14] For much more on this, see John Drane, *Do Christians know how to be Spiritual? The rise of New Spirituality and the Mission of the Church*: the 2004 London Lectures in Contemporary Christianity (London: Darton Longman & Todd, 2005).

When I was teaching theology (in a Divinity faculty that was supposedly equipping people for Christian ministry!) I soon learned that it was not possible to use biblical analogies without explanation, as most young people had no idea about the content of basic Bible stories. Those who teach subjects like English literature and Philosophy struggle with the same reality, for many historic texts in those disciplines incorporate references to biblical themes which are no longer part of the worldview of otherwise well-read students.

At the same time, there is enormous interest in Jesus as a celebrity figure. One of the best-selling books of the day is Dan Brown's *The DaVinci Code*, which is in effect an exploration of the 'secret life' of Jesus, asking if his 'public' image matched his 'private' reality. Millions of people have read it, and are so fascinated by its alleged revelations that Rosslyn Chapel has had to employ extra staff to cope with the flood of visitors who have visited searching for the Holy Grail.

Widespread ignorance of how to speak of Jesus

To understand *The DaVinci Code*, readers have to consider complex historical arguments, and become familiar with arcane vocabulary that they would not otherwise be interested in, so it is not possible to claim that as a society we are afraid of hard work. But why is it that the authentic story of Jesus is not greeted with such enthusiasm? Could it be that we do not know how to speak of Jesus in a celebrity culture, even though he is by any definition one of the greatest celebrities in the entire history of the world? Have we lost sight of the fascinating personality revealed in the New Testament and reduced him to a bundle of theoretical ideas and abstract concepts, when we could be presenting him as a living, breathing person whose career was indeed shot through with the same sort of ambivalence that so fascinates us in today's celebrity lifestyles?

I am constantly amazed by the strong negative feelings that can be evoked among Christians when it is suggested that as well as being an object of devotion, Jesus ought also to be a model for everyday living—a real, accessible celebrity.

∾

Finally, there are some aspects of celebrity culture that do not accord with the values of the gospel. For example, while the emphasis on experimentation through dress and lifestyle can be offered as a way for people to escape convention and explore their own personal freedom, in another sense 'it enslaves people in the necessity of developing an image, striking a pose, constructing identity through style, forcing people to worry about how they dress and look and how other people will react to their image.'[15]

Sometimes it will be appropriate to take action about such things through the democratic systems that are available to us. Mostly, though, it will be a more costly business of journeying with people as they work out who and what may be worth following as a model for life in all its fullness. They are unlikely to take our word for it, because we no longer live in the world of Christendom, when the church had an automatic right to speak on any topic it chose, and to be heeded. We are called to be more vulnerable, to share the good news not from positions of strength but out of the weakness that is our own fragile existence.

Post-moderns suspect that many things are not what they seem, something that resonates as a major theme in the teaching of Jesus,

---

[15] Douglas Kellner, *Media Culture* (London: Routledge. 1995), p. 285.

which is another reason why just telling the story is going to be a major component in any effective Christian engagement with celebrity culture.

Books from
Rutherford House

the *WayMark* series

Human Rights

its culture & other moral confusions

by Howard Taylor

This incisive and provocative book examines the gradual development of the relatively new 'human rights culture' which is already dominating much thinking in our European society to the detriment of an earlier culture in which human responsibilities were rightly acknowledged.

Readers will be challenged to ask whether human rights legislation ought to be the sole means of judging the rightness or wrongness of the legislation of national governments; and whether the growing human rights culture, in encouraging each to claim his or her own rights, is adversely affecting our society.

£4.00

Rutherford House
17 Claremont Park, Edinburgh, EH6 7PJ

the *WayMark* series

Counsellors & Counselling
An Introductory Guide
By Noel Due

'While this book is not on how to counsel, it does lay out the case for counselling and what counselling can and cannot achieve. The author aims to help those involved in counselling situations understand the ways in which pastors, psychologists and psychiatrists have sought to grapple with the contribution of psychological studies and theological reflection on the human condition.

'The freshness of his approach, the familiarity with the British and American cultures and the freedom from obscurantism make this book a balanced and informative guide to the many strands in the fabric of the modern counselling movement.'

Dr Montagu Barker, Consultant Psychiatrist

£4.00

Rutherford House

sales@rutherfordhouse.org.uk
www.rutherfordhouse.org.uk
0131 554 1206

Other Rutherford House Publications

Pastoral Visitation
A Pocket Manual
by David Short & David Searle

An indispensable aid for all engaged in pastoral visitation; with Scripture texts, brief comments, prayers and devotional verses for use in every kind of situation.

The Gospel of John
Pastoral & Theological Studies
by Ronald S Wallace

Scholarly comment, devotional reflection, pastoral application and topical relevance seamlessly combine in this excellent volume. Eminently accessible to the housewife, the student and the theological untrained reader, it is also a most useful tool for the pastor and the preacher.

Both books are £7.50 if ordered direct from

Rutherford House
0131 554 1206
sales@rutherfordhouse.org.uk

Two books by George M Philip

Journey with God
Daily Devotional Readings
through the book of Exodus
£6.00

Faith in the Dark
Daily Devotional Readings
through the book of Job
£5.00

and then there were nine...
the ten commandments
in daily living
by David Searle

'Pastoral and prophetic, clear and convicting, David Searle's gentle survey of God's blockbusting ten commandments overflows with truth and wisdom. I would like to see it made compulsory reading for all church members.'   *J.I. Packer*

£6.00